Volcanic Interruptions

Poems by Adela Najarro

Paintings by Janet Trenchard

Cover: Janet Trenchard, "Momotombo," acrylic/mixed media.

Copyright © 2023 Adela Najarro & Janet Trenchard
ISBN: 978-1-7332415-8-8
Published by Jamii Publishing
San Bernandino, CA
www.JamiiPublishing.com
All rights reserved.

Fourteen volcanos rise
in my remembered country
in my mythical country.
Fourteen volcanos of foliage and stone
where strange clouds hold back
the screech of a homeless bird.
Who said that my country was green?
— Claribel Alegría
From "Flowers from the Volcano"
(Translation Carolyn Forché)

Volcanic Interruptions combines the poetry of Adela Najarro with the acrylic/ mixed media paintings by Janet Trenchard. As feminists, both artists want to depict how a woman's power arises from the earth, soil, and volcanoes, and they have been collaborating on this theme throughout the Covid-19 pandemic.

In this chapbook, Najarro's poems and Trenchard's paintings dialog about the feminine as power and life force, where volatility is strength and symbolized through the theme of vulcanism. Najarro's poems and Trenchard's paintings draw on vibrant earth energy so that the written word and image come together in coversation. In addition, theirs is a fiery collaboration between cultures where Latinx and White coexist, harmonize, and create a vision for a world where the vitality of women is highlighted in art.

We hope you enjoy exploring how the poems and the paintings broil and bubble in the fire of feminine volcanic energy.

Contents

Poems

Chantico Swings	3
Before the Volcano Blows	4
Chantico Flames	7
Looking Under Tombstones on Día de los Muertos	8
Lamentation for Papi	10
Los Volcánes de Nicaragua	12
Below the Momotombo Volcano	15
Volcanic Poetics	17
After the Volcano Ate the Moon	19

Paintings

Chantico Swings	1
Momotombo II	6
Ancestors	9
Bitter Green	11
Chantico's Place	14
Origenes	16
Embers	21

Acknowledgements	23
About the Author and Artist	24

"Chantico Swings," Acrylic/Mixed Media

Chantico Swings

She doesn't speak German, English
nor Spanish. She is prior to the four directions,
prior to Sandino, Somoza, US Marines, AK-47s,
cocaine, and communists.

She is queen of the underworld
inside the Masaya crater.
After bathing in the fires of a lava lake,
she dances on red hot boulders.

When she drinks foaming elixirs,
séance tables rise and tambourines
sound the failed heartbeats of the dead.

Sometimes when the dead are too chatty,
she opens a bottle of Flor de Caña so that all
will have breath sweetened with rum.

Before Pan Am flights out of Managua
landed in San Francisco,
Chantico was one of many girls.
Then she trembled and the plaster wall
joining her bedroom to the kitchen
cracked, bricks tumbled.

She was a woman now.
After a swill of methane, she exhales
like Marlene Dietrich,
but only smoke remains.

Before the Volcano Blows

I will speak Spanish
to many stray dogs with fleas
and find my way

to a nameless street
where angels spoke
to my mother as a girl.

Momotombo will simmer
its vengeful breath
rumbling and roaring
in the background.

It will be a simple matter,
by then,
to stand at the edge
of a world gone mad

since all the secrets
will have been released
into the rainforest canopy
between Managua and León.

The few vowels left
will explode from parrots squawking
and truth will rain down
upon all who accompany

the poor and tired
endlessly scratching memories.

This is all because of my mother's whispers
and that I can never remember
her exact birthday.

Was it on the 22nd or the 28th
that she broke into the world
with a cacophony of lament

and taught me to hide within the walls
of my own deception?

Too many have withstood
the cataclysm of broken doors,
the harangue of voices
that never cease, the visceral schema
of too much that has come before.

When I finally arrive
with my own broken being
packed tight
in a worn leather bag,

I will not cry into satin blankets.

Instead, I will sip mint tea
with two ice cubes slowly melting
as my hair curls
into ash and dust.

"Momotombo II," Acrylic/Mixed Media

Chantico Flames

When looking up saints and goddesses
that crackle through soil
in a homeland I've only seen once,

I found Chantico Inn & Suites, Chantico Global,
Chantico Fire, corporate fumes
smoldering from the goddess,
her home, hearth, and volcanic royal

menstrual blood. Chiconahui Itzcuintli
sent warriors into battle who prayed
she would bathe their hearts in fire.

No longer. Chantico, simply a name
for a Starbucks six ounce chocolate drink
with a pinch of cayenne. Her heat, her fire,
flows through every woman's veins.

We bleed lava lakes. We are Gaia.
But not strong enough to melt conquistador helmets,
chainmail, and swords.

The Telica eruption couldn't take out Somoza's eldest son.
He kept riding a stallion through black lava sand.
Girls hiding blood stains on panties
stopped speaking as parrots mocked
them from treetops.

My mother didn't marry Reynoldo nor build
a mini-mall with a hair salon,
fashion emporium, and an agua frescas quick stop.

My mother came here. Learned English. Sent me
to college. Chola? Cholita? Chiconahui,
Chicona, Chingona? Now Chantico turns up

in different cities spouting flames as she speaks
in broken tongues. With ruby lips, she stacks

paper bags into a red Ford Fiesta.

Looking Under Tombstones
on Día de los Muertos

My ancestors are women without men.
> The men drank themselves into shivering skeletons.

My ancestors are women without men.
> The men ran away into other lives,
> only to drink themselves hollow.

My ancestors are women without men.
> The men did not know what to do
> with these creatures that brought life to sons and daughters,
> so they began mixing whiskey with honey laced water.

My ancestors are women without men.
> The men desired bosoms, tender hearts, tight hips,
> but couldn't stay with the pulsing psychic connection
> emitted from a vagina in love,
> so they opened dusty bottles of 40 proof liquor.

My ancestors are women without men
> because the men were overwhelmed
> by the power of vaginas, amplified breasts,
> and the ecstatic visage of a woman in love at the height of orgasm.
> They began to drink, then run, from one caldera to the next
> dodging the ballistic boulders sent shooting across sky by goddesses.

My ancestors are women
who stand at the rim of volcanoes
and issue forth magma fountains.
They ignite air, sea, land and sky
into lightning, thunder, tornadoes, and hurricanes.

"Ancestors," Acrylic/Mixed Media

Lamentation for Papi

My father grew up under a verdant jungle sky
and inhaled ash from erupting volcanoes.
He listened to el perico verde de Nicaragua.
She always told him what he had done wrong.
My father chewed limes with salt since he knew bitter times.
My father sliced olives into arroz con pollo and was happy.
He never bit a red apple, only the green one Eve handed
him from the nightstand before she turned off the lights.
My father was grassy green lust that loved platanos fritos.
The jungles of his youth, smoldering calderas, and the perico verde
stole all the limes, olives, and apples.
My father became a broken green couch, old from too much wear.
My father wore a green bathrobe over a white v-neck t-shirt
and striped pajama bottoms.
On his feet were worn brown leather slippers.
He picked dried green leaves from artificial carnations.
After a simple lunch, he faded into a light green afternoon
and left three platanos in a bowl on the kitchen table.

"Bitter Green," Cold Wax & Oil

Los Volcánes de Nicaragua

—for my father

Cosigüina: North

North only North—no trails, steep slopes.
Stand at the rim of the crater,
pour your mother out:

The mother who left you in Managua.
The mother who brought you to the States.

San Cristóbal Volcano: Travel

St. Christopher is not a saint
but a martyr   protects nevertheless.

Planes and visas take so many North,
then REVOLUCIÓN:
trucks lined with palm fronds,
everyone celebrates.

Cerro Negro Volcano: Hills

Except you.   You liked Somoza, the dictator,
the special contracts, the ability
to sit in a hotel,
order a steak with red wine reduction,
mushrooms in a cream sauce,
prawns bathed in butter.

Did you sand board down the slope
of an active volcano?

El Hoyo: Emptiness

If your mother leaves
and doesn't come back,
are you left on the edge of a volcano?
Will you keep jumping into lava
to burn away the loss?
Will love feel like heat
for the rest of your life?

Momotombo: Energy

Managua with its geothermal plant
at the base of the volcano
is like a woman undressing
for the first time.

So many women.
So many times.

Apoyeque: Sulfur

Volcanoes in a chain
are like generations

one after the other
that keep doing
the same thing:

combustion, volatile gases,
the tremble of tectonic plates crashing.

Except, I mean bodies
with other bodies.

Except, I mean feeding
the body with other bodies

until then there is

only ash.

"Chantico's Place," Acrylic/Mixed Media

Below the Momotombo Volcano

Whenever the gods and goddess' of volcanoes meet up for a barbeque, they gather at Chantico's place. Her fat iron wood stove breathes fire. The first to show up are always the dwarfs and giants. They rise out of Icelandic snow with a tremble and shake, then lug in coolers filled with vodka shooters. Hephaestus is a little late. He brings the tea set and silverware having turned rage into art in his studio at a prominent address on Piccadilly Square. Heph is still steaming after being conceived by pure female juju and thrown off a cliff. He went free falling for 24 hours. Even though he landed on his feet, he never could walk right. Out back by the cascading red flowers of the banana trees, Vulcan sets up Tiki torches to keep away the buzz. There's a Twitter feed on him about complicity in forging lances for conquistadores, Remington rifles for US Yankee banana companies, and AK-47's for the School of the Americas. It's rumored he had a hand in welding jeeps, grenades, high speed bullets, and landmines for Somoza. He did the same for the Sandinistas, the same for the Contras, the same for this army, for that army. Vulcan doesn't discriminate. Anywhere heat is needed to forge a cause of destruction, he's willing to oblige. But he's so long winded and never gets to the point that in order to cope, Mt. St. Helens begins to layer charcoal while Pele pulls out a Zippo lighter. The women spark an idea while tending the barbeque smoke and flames. Why not create a train of volcanoes so that each child born on Central American soil will carry the power of fire in their left pinky? It can begin with an Aztec mother drying corn. After she ascends the slopes of Momotombo for flame to heat el comal, a freckle will be born of fire and from then on all children of the Americas will carry an affinity for the left and all that burns.

"Origenes," Acrylic/Mixed Media

Volcanic Poetics

After the soldiers left
bullet holes and torn mattresses,

after iguanas ran off with the sun,
after pericos emerged violently squawking,

after the dictator collected
music boxes and skulls,

a song rose from the stink
of a river festering yellow mud

where one eye of a crocodile
watched you, I, we, todos

break bones, break bodies.
I want to tell you about after,

how bones knit, courage rises,
and we stave off despair.

Once in that country filled with mango trees,
where sharks live in fresh water,

where monkeys are kept on leashes,
where the ice cream is salty,

el ministro de Cultura issued
a call to language

as action, a call to write poems
about ordinary objects

and Exteriorismo began stirring
a pot of beans, adding

oil and then left over rice,
to make gallo pinto. A plain dish

that Danny likes, a child, our child,
here in the States with Nica blood.

Poems are his legacy,
along with a lava-filled past

that percolated a revolution
of sound, vida, and ranas,

ranitas, little froggies on a farm
on the road to Momotombo.

My mother's words
explode volcanic vowels.

¡Ay! ¡Cómo queman!
The slow burn down

the side of a mountain
with its top blown off.

Nature on fire. Poetry
a living thing.

After the Volcano Ate the Moon

It was dark. The bike did not have reflectors.
I did not have a helmet, but I went anyway.

When I approached a car pulling out of a driveway

with a — *Hey, Hey, I'm here. I'm here,*

a man in an Audi retorted that I should get a light.
Since I didn't like his tone of voice,

the volcano ate him. I was doing good.

I had cleared the road and was on the bike path.
The trail was smooth and divided
by a yellow line. I stayed on my side.

The meadow was to my right
and there were bushes here and there:
dwarf pines rippled in wind.

Since I thought the trees were pretty,
right after I rode past their quivering,

the volcano ate them.

I was riding fast, wind massaging my hair,
and still I thought the moon would arrive
at any moment. I didn't hit a stray rock and fall.

The volcano had eaten them all.

I stayed on the trail and passed two women with a dog
and another woman jogging,
music seeping out from her head phones.

When the dog barked at the non-existent moon,
the volcano ate it.

Then she ate the women.

I noticed stars lit the night sky,
but the moon still had not appeared
and the trail had mysteriously emptied.

A deep blue stillness arose
from the mountain.

I began to think about the volcano,
about how rocks within rocks
melt down to magma.

All the rumble and rage.
How heat and passion
flow down a mountainside.

The beauty of glass formed
as a volcano weeps, then
the dry edge of volcanic rock.

How the last time,
the sky thundered
a suffocating ash,

I stepped over a molten river,

and burst into flower and song.

"Embers" Acrylic/Mixed Media

Acknowledgements

"Volcanic Poetics" and "Before the Volcano Blows." *The Rumpus,* September 9th, 2021.

"Los Volcánes de Nicaragua." *Anacua Literary Arts Journal ~ Migrations,* 2019.

"Lamentations for Papi." *Aurora Poetry,* Volume 2, 2019.

"Chantico Swings." *Nimrod International Journal,* Awards 40, 2018.

"Barbecue below the Momotombo Volcano" as "What Happened at the Barbecue below the Momotombo Volcano." *Catamaran Literary Reader,* 2018.

"Chantico Flames" as "Los Volcánes de Nicaragua." *Written Here: The Community of Writers Poetry Review 2016.* Squaw Valley, 2016.

"Looking Under Tombstones on Día de los Muertos" as "Día de los Muertos." *Soñadores: We Came to Dream.* Ed. Odilia Galván Rodríguez. Canto Hondo/Deep Song Books, 2016.

About the Author and Artist

Adela Najarro

Adela Najarro, whose extended family emigrated from Nicaragua, is the author of three poetry collections: *Split Geography*, *Twice Told Over* and *My Childrens*, a chapbook with teaching resources. With *My Childrens* she hopes to bring poetry into the classroom so that students can explore creative writing, identity, and what it means to be Latinx in US society. She teaches at Cabrillo College. Adela holds a doctorate in literature and creative writing from Western Michigan University, as well as an M.F.A. from Vermont College. She is widely published in numerous anthologies and literary magazines. More information about Adela can be found at her website: www.adelanajarro.com.

Janet Trenchard

Janet Trenchard has exhibited around the San Francisco Bay Area and has had work in statewide juried shows. She has been a member of Gallery House in Palo Alto, Gallery 24 in Los Gatos, and the Santa Cruz Art League for many years. She also has participated in Santa Cruz Open Studios, the Santa Cruz Virtual Artists Network, and Pajaro Valley Arts. Janet has taught several workshops at the Santa Cruz Art League and loves the hubbub of creativity that is teaching. She taught art in the Eastside Union High School District in San Jose before retiring to pursue her own art fulltime.